Pebbles in the Sand of Life

Reflections in Poetry

Richard Bohnet

Ken & Mary Lou
Hope you enjoy!
Richard Bohnet

Pebbles in the Sand of Life
Reflections in Poetry
by Richard Bohnet

ISBN 978-1-5323-2323-2

1. Poetic memoir; 2. Life reflections

Front Cover: Jeanne Bohnet Coyhis

Edited by: Richard Simonelli

To order books contact:

Richard Bohnet
400 Clocktower Ridge Drive Apt. 317
Winchester VA 22603
rbohnet@verizon.net

Pebbles in the Sand of Life

Richard Bohnet

Dedication

This book is dedicated to my daughter, Jeanne Bohnet Coyhis, and her husband, Don Coyhis for offering to use the publishing capabilities that Coyhis Publishing Company has in place to realize my dream to see my poetic reflections put into print.

Many people have asked me through the years, "When are you going to publish?" I have felt that it would not be possible to have that happen. Therefore, I have deflected those comments, while secretly holding out the hope. Through Jeanne's efforts, my dream has turned into reality.

To my family and friends who, over the years, have inspired me, and to those who have made this book possible, this is the result. **I thank you!**

Richard Bohnet
September, 2016

Foreword

This muse of poetry lay dormant and undiscovered within me until age 37. I had read poetry, but never thought of writing, until one weekend at a Church Retreat in the mountains of West Virginia, on land that had a river running through the property. I wrote my first poem The River, a mixture of joy and some fantasy. I shared it that night with those on the retreat and got positive feedback. That did it!

What a way of getting pent up feelings out and the freedom was amazing. That very Christmas, I put my own poem on blank Christmas cards, and have been enclosing verses in Christmas cards every year since. Christmas has always been special and sharing perspectives through the years has been a real joy.

I have found the subject matter to be virtually inexhaustible. In this book is a compendium of my works through the years. There is a loose separation in the divisions that I have chosen. Christmas and Travel speak for themselves, but the Journey of Life, for me, speaks the loudest.

I hope that you will find enjoyment, along with many other emotions, as you traverse this humble book.

– Richard Bohnet

September, 2016

Contents

Christmas Poems

– 1–

THE GIFT

The prayer, was peace,
The way, by love.
Expectancy, on words of old
Now fulfilled! O fragile babe -
The wonder of a simple birth.

In Bethlehem, a stable yet,
Hovering star, scarcely seen,
Sage and shepherd touched.
A world in an instant moved
Same again, never to be
A gift for all humanity.

Christmas, 1971
(My very first Christmas poem)

– 2–

CHRISTMAS HOPE – 1973

People adrift in leaderless sea,
Desire for an inward flee.
Crises crowd the daily scene
Power used, abused excessively.
At times deluging complexity,
Able minds lack humanity.
Basic structures lack relevancy,
Right or wrong – are left unclear.

Through time a chorus clearly foretold,
And heavenly visit to virgin, behold!
A guiding star, abruptly bold
Magi and shepherds by visions were told.
The humble stable manger – so old.
And God in human form, like gold.

Its message then, just as now,
Eternal hope and heaven sent love'
Since Jesus' life was what God gave.
Wholeness with which to make our life,
Each human unique and with esteem
Salvation has been personified.
Man now redeemed and dignified.

Christmas, 1973

– 3–

THE APPROACHING DAY

Catalogs and gentle hints,
Shopping crowded, festive stores.
Rushing, brushing, gift bags filled,
Daily baking of cookies and cakes.
Color streaks on trees and eaves.
Assembled crèche, the spotlight takes.
Finding, buying, a shapely pine.
Ribbon and wreath brighten the door.
Candles and greens with Christmas décor.

Anthems sung and The Story we hear.
Church aglow, flickering with cheer.
Secrets that each can hardly hold.
Traditional dinner, all dressed up.
Hands held, heads bowed in prayer.
Turkey, trimmings, and fancy molds.
Well known carols fill the room.
Stockings now tacked on fireplace.
Tree; still bare, set in its place.

By now excitement overflows,
Glance outside to check the snow,
Christmas, its joy, once more bestows.

Christmas, 1973

– 4–

DAVID AND AMOS

David and Amos, brothers of ten,
Roaming the fields, just like the men,
Their father, among others, are tending their flocks,
The boys busy climbing and scrambling on rocks
Learning their trade, through long hot days
To keep accurate count and search for strays.

After every desert night fall.
Cold damp mist hovers over all,
Shepherds come close around the fire,
Singing of work, life and desire.
The brothers too, participate.
Absorbing culture, hearing fate.

At times while the brothers were alone,
Time singing folk songs with rich high tone,
In happy diversion, knowing time well spent
These two harmonize a unique talent.
But all too soon there's work to do.
Find a lamb that is lost, help one brand new.

Then came a night that filled all with wonder.
Light bright as day, rumbles of thunder.
The shepherds startled; recoiling in fear,
Then angels praising God, abruptly appear.
Announcing the Birth on this night of nights
Point to the hovering star so bright.

(continued)

DAVID AND AMOS (continued)

Shepherds entrance and forsaking their sheep,
Even David and Amos arise with a leap,
The multitude surges to Bethlehem town,
Curious about this new King of our own.
And there beneath the followed star beam
Bathed its light on this quaint manger scene.

All fell to their knees in worshipful pose,
Then David and Amos suddenly arose,
And slowly approached the Babe in repose.
A gift for the Savior through teary eyed gaze.
Their voices in lilting harmony raise,
The “Celebration of Life” in musical praise.

Christmas, 1974

– 5–

THE FLIGHT

The warning dream in the night,
Directed Joseph's straightway flight.
With infant Jesus and Mary, too.
Beyond the reach of Herod, who
Fearful and impassioned for his power
Sought to destroy God's precious flower.

Precipitate voyage blurring day to night,
Spanning miles to bring calm from fright.
Always the direction of an unseen hand
Parents, Babe and beast, a pitiful band.
Threading through towns and craggy crust,
Oppressive sun and sirocco's dust.

Fortnight's progress to banks of Nile,
Safe haven for rest and waiting awhile.
Far from Bethlehem and Herod's wrath,
Innocent young, a tragic bloodbath.
Jeremiah's dark forecast fulfilled
Wailing and weeping would not be stilled.

The Lord in a dream, touched Joseph in bed
"Arise and return, Herod is dead."
A joyous retracing of the arduous way.
Called out of Egypt, the prophet would say.
Then directed to Nazareth in Galilee,
To grow and be the revelation of Thee.

Christmas, 1975

– 6–

REFLECTIONS OF WONDER

Now the preparing is through,
Materially, no more to do.
Reflect the import of Christmas day,
Why pick this oasis of blue,
When through the whole of creation,
On endless other specks of dust
God could have appeared
And blessed their eternity.
Somehow this was not to be –
I wonder why?

How a birth so long ago
Forever altered history.
Likely never to cease.
For humans can now know
The uniqueness of this birth.
He strode the path we must tread,
Willing an existential guide:
The meaning of being a Me.
Healing of body and soul,
Love of psyche and thou,
A healthy passion for Jehovah.
Salvation and heavenly grace,
Glimpses of what lies beyond.
An attainment of eternity.
Is there a reason why?

Just give a thankful prayer
For a sharing extremely rare,
The gift that is ever there.

Christmas, 1975

– 7–

THE SAVIOR'S VIEW

Well I've arrived in a primitive way,
Umbilical cord, chewed, and I lay,
In a makeshift bed of wood and hay.
My roughhewn blanket wraps tender skin,
Mother Mary cradles me within,
Nurses and nourishes and kisses my chin.

Starlight bathes the floor around me,
Shepherds and boys gathered adoringly,
Even Magi come to express their glee,
In the night, unaccountably forced to flee
Hard, frightening, sleepless journey,
Quiet growth goes on at the river Nile.
As Divine suborned to the human for a while.

Like the living soul I am; I learn and grow.
But something soon calls; takes me in tow,
The God within, His seeds soon sow,
And I am driven, my Maker to know.
Apart even beyond Joseph and Mary's domain.
I travel a path, so filled with pain.
Three short years teaching, is all I sustain.
And after Palm Sunday's too quick reign,
Find for me, alas both Calvary and rain.
Suffering alone mortal sins, enduring the pain,
So all humanity, forever, unshackled from chains.

Christmas, 1976

– *8*–

NO ROOM IN THE INN

After Caesar's arbitrary decree,
Brought Joseph and Mary to Galilee,
Amid the multitude, admittedly unfree
And she about ready, a mother to be.

How could anyone in truth have known
A resting place could not be found
In this bulging insensitive town.
Forcing these humans to lie on the ground.

Among the beasts of God's creation
Mary labored with God's gestation
Brought forth the divine declaration
Human embodiment of Holy revelation.

We fervently pray that we not be
As callous as Innkeepers of Galilee
And find no room within our Me;
To open our hearts to the truth of Thee.

Christmas, 1976

– 9–

NIGHT OF NIGHTS

Moonbeams dancing on straw strewn floor
Cold light penetrates the darkened door
Beasts shuffle and stir and a muted roar,
Huddling humans shivering and damp,
Lonely within, heightened by dying lamp.
Tears and beads fill Mary's young face,
Feels Joseph's tender cradled embrace.
Cry of new life in suddenness fills,
As Christ delivered; the planet stills.
Watchful shepherds throughout nearby hills,
Visited in brilliance fears and chills
Obeying the starlight transfixed there,
While Bethlehem slumbers, none are aware.

This night of nights transcending display
God has produced a passion filled play.

Christmas, 1977

– 10 –

MIGHT I HAVE BEEN

Might I have been that Virgin blessed
By God; alone among women
To bear a heavenly burden.
And risk my name and life,
So ancient prophets' words
Might totally be fulfilled.

Might I have been foul King Herod,
By power and vice corrupt,
Who so much feared a humble birth,
That his baseness took control.
In a vain attack on God
That only hastened his demise.

Might I have been a lonesome shepherd,
Existing in simplicity.
Aware of elemental things,
Open to stars and angel songs.
Running, curious to the new child King.
To worship, perceive, and believe.

Might I have been an Eastern King,
Blessed with all worldly knowledge,
So sure that his life was inchoate.
That he came; a seeker from afar,
Questing for a higher King,
Exchanging worldly, for lasting gifts.

(continued}

MIGHT I HAVE BEEN (continued}

Might I have been of the multitude,
Put upon, coping, and weary.
Strangers force to ancestral homes,
To ease the oppressors' control.
Eye glazed; and spirits unaware,
Indifferent to God, made flesh.

Might I have been a stalwart Roman,
Behind temporal power supreme.
Civilized and conquering nation,
Proud with status and given rights.
Many gods demand their due,
To assure that Rome stays eternal.

Somewhere—right there – was I
And you?

Christmas, 1978

– 11 –

YOU SAY YOU DON'T LIKE CHRISTMAS

You say you don't like Christmas,
Too commercialized – too sterilized.
Stores ornamented by mid-October,
And catalogs pushed upon you.
Each year's set of banal songs,
Countless specials that clutter TV.
Santa Claus's everywhere,
Gaudy lights and ersatz trees,
And so much focus on getting.
In Xmas, the X is unknown.

You may be right, but ---
Energy surges from the opposite view....
A reaching out to those in need,
Care and thought given to gifts,
Arranging to have loved ones near.
Sprouting candles showering a warm glow,
Choosing, adorning, the perfect tree,
Cakes and cookies, hot and crisp,
Haunting choruses of "O Holy Night."
An electric expectancy in the air,
Feeling the joy, embodied in Christ.
Sensing, above all, a surge of love,
Some moments when living has meaning.

Christmas, 1978

– 12 –

CHRIST AS SYMBOL

The primitives with simple fears
Of earth, wind, flood and fire
Worshiping the imponderable
These gods of daily survival.

Mind develops, division occurs
More gods filling more needs
Harvest, rain, illness, and blight,
Homage to power and mystery.

Civilization, culture and growth
More major and demigods
Personified through myths
Touching a diverse inner life.

Bursting of the Judeo creation
All gods have grown to One,
Power, omniscience, a mighty judge,
Obeyed to gain eternal reward.

Still the human psyche craves more
And what is that desire to be.
God, a coming, incarnation
For certain all mankind agrees.

So comes convergence of history,
Of angels, a virgin, and signs,
Zodiac, expectancy, and birth.
This man-god symbol explodes.

(continued)

CHRIST AS SYMBOL (continued)

Through all, the simple truth remains,
That Christ shared our common plight,
A clear example of meaning
Of life here and beyond the light.

So this God of all creation
And the Christ that gave man hope,
And joined in a timeless fashion,
In a fiery spreading word.

Christmas, 1980

– 13 –

THE ADVENT CALENDAR

The light that pierces darkness is day one,
The King among Kings—the prophets foretold,
Isaiah's son of God –bright as the sun.
Mary hears a heavenly voice of gold.
Mourning doves flutter and soared above her,
Spirit thus implanted within her soul,
Acceptance of a fateful hereafter,
Day eight, recalls Elizabeth's role.
Planets and stars in unique conjunction,
Triggered the search from out of the East,
Caesars' decree to count population,
Day twelve; finds Joseph and Mary on beast.
All alone in cold crowded Bethlehem
And see a frail woman great with child.
Angels practicing a joyous anthem
Against a dark Herod's mind, racing wild.
Celestial display gives shepherds a call,
Through a sky ringing with music and song,
Mixing fear with joy, a race to the stall
This night is electric. What could go wrong?
The cosmos alive on twenty-fourth day
Worldly kings, worship and adoration.
A heavenly glow bathes the manger way,
Triumphant trio at God's creation.

Christmas, 1981

– 14 –

CHRIST, MARY, JOSEPH

My dear Christ, Savior unborn
Sweet Mary, Virgin serene,
O' Joseph, so strong, yet scared.
To this mystic unknown, by faith directed,
Angels and dreams, and events unexpected.

My dear Christ, tiny and bare,
Sweet Mary, with tender care,
O' Joseph, grateful in prayer.
Far from Bethlehem's streets, and human tempest,
God's gift of love in a manger so modest.

My dear Christ, fisher of me,
Sweet Mary, great majesty
O' Joseph, a sturdy tree.
From the shores of the Nile, to hot Galilee
Prophecy and signs, that the world cannot see.

My dear Christ, truths brand new,
Sweet Mary, her wisdom grew,
O' Joseph, his wood to hew.
A heavenly chord strikes a human refrain,
Miracles of healing, and freeing life's pain.

My dear Christ, God's perfection,
Sweet Mary, introspection,
O' Joseph, far distant cheer.
Tumult and turmoil, as the climax neared,
Betrayed and denied, and the cross to be bared.

(continued)

CHRIST, MARY, JOSEPH (continued)

My dear Christ, the Way made clear
Sweet Mary, a heavy fear,
O' Joseph, far distant cheer,
To this mystic unknown, by faith directed,
Dying and angels and life resurrected!

Christmas, 1982

– *15* –

THE BARN

Cold and quiet twinkling night,
Crusty snow and a needle mat,
Thick and black, imposing height,
Lightly crowned with a misty hat.

And there upon a rolling lea,
An aging, worn, ramshackle barn,
Near a massive, majestic tree.
Passionately tuned, I am drawn.

To barely perceptible sound
And a glimmer of candle light
Round rays on rusty roof rebound.
A lonely white owl flaps in flight.

For a moment my soul takes flight,
And hovers in the tall black tree.
The barn below, now bathed in light.
Suddenly, a small voice made free.

Lilting fresh noise, where none was heard,
Stirring and throbbing from the woods,
Jumbled rise of excited words
Pointing to where a King now stood.

By now I reach the barn alone.
The peeling paint and half gone door,
The sights and sounds have somehow flown,
Only a dream could now restore.

Christmas, 1992

– 16 –

HOME

In some distant place, some distant space,
I make a life, in my own way, each day.
Known to myself and the friends I embrace,
Through a persona, I choose to display.

How far from my beginning, I have come,
Hard to know if I continue to grow.
Can I pause? Look inward; what I've become.
Can I hold the tide? Do I want to know?

It's said you cannot return anymore,
To your roots, your center, your own being.
Not true. That journey, I can still explore,
This trek I'm making, is surely freeing.

Now this cold, starry, northern, winter night.
Vibrating voices carry in the air.
Glowing tree, dressed in festive green and white,
And affirming sparks, those assembled, share.

Its Beginning; it was a break with the past.
Whether I'm here in body or spirit,
It's the Life, the example that will last.
My home, and I never want to leave it.

Christmas, 1994

– 17 –

LIGHTED LAMPS

A winter's night without a moon,
Tiny heavenly lights are strewn,
Time is what you want it to be,
A silence the land and sea.

The season is right and sages await,
A savior from this worldly weight,
While most commoners still struggle;
Unconscious hope yet to untangle.

For in this Birth; one night, one time,
Fulfilled prophecy, reason, and rhyme.
One extraordinary life,
Shared our feelings, hope and strife.

Then for a while the lights went dim
And in the air a plaintive hymn.
Creatures felt a deepened grief.
A spark had blazed ever so brief.

Yet the feelings were not bereft,
For the lighted lamps that were left,
Took hold in the afterglow,
And became a rolling psychic flow.

Mans' way of thinking had grown old.
Broke now forever, this mortal mold
With ideas so utterly bold.
Redemption, love, eternal soul.

Christmas, 1997

– 18 –

MEETING JESUS

If I had been in time and space,
Abroad in the land where a Birth takes place,
That was foretold, but to most unknowing,
Would I have reacted to rumors,
And searched for the baby King,
Or scoffed with the legions
That let no belief enter in.
Would my kin have escaped Herod's scourge,
Or might I have lost precious fruit.

And then all those empty years
A lifetime of struggle for me.
Where burdens of my existence,
Pushes hope to edges of my mind,

Then a star ignites again,
After years of journey and flights,
He, and his band walk this land.
In the twilight of my life
A desperation gnaws me still.

(continued)

MEETING JESUS (continued)

And this life with little to lose,
Might change if stories are true.
Perhaps this man will lead the way
To remove hated Roman slavery.
I struggle to follow the crowd,
Straining to hear, silent from afar.
Word so fresh, the mind sets to spin.
Hope fills the heart, and anxiety too.
What does it all mean?
Moving closer, and closer still,
I peer in those eyes, deep cool pools,
And the voice, strong and peaceful calm.
I am drawn in, releasing control.
All too soon, it comes to an end.
Drifting home with my senses filled
Aware of the buzz from all that heard,
This teacher, these teachings;
Within me now there is a seed.
The question is; Will I heed?

Christmas, 1997

– 19 –

MYSTICAL MAGIC

The snow crunches and the limb sprays,
This rotund spirit, this Santa Claus.
Starts a journey at the sun's last rays,
To cover the world; no time to pause.

Down chim'nies, through doors, skimming a wall,
Walking, flying. And bounding about.
A bulging sack, no problem at all.
Precarious, but nothing falls out.

Videos, clothes, skateboards, small trains,
Trees lit, full stockings, brightly wrapped toys.
Job done, he's gone, as the night sky wanes,
Leaving twinkles on girls; smiles on boys.

This magic, you ask. "How can it be?"
It defies any explanation.
Yet, if you believe, and have eyes to see
It's a true mystical celebration.

Christmas, 1998

– 20 –

CHRISTMAS SHADOW BOX

A Christmas cat, how about that,
Ribboned and sitting on a mat.
Mistletoe, you know what that means,
Lots of kisses and hugs, unseen.
A pear tree where a partridge sits,
A true love's gift that surely fits.
Tinkling bell on a young pine tree,
Symbol of joy, when we are free.
A golden horn, asserting "Noel".
Proclaims! Exclaims! That all is well.
A sprig of holly, a morning dove,
Some think it's peace, others feel love,
Candy filled stockings, Christmas Eve,
Santa's gift to those who believe.
A Christmas ball, molded by hand,
Part of an illusion that's grand.
A mandolin sits and it longs
For someone to release its songs.
Brightly wrapped gifts, filling a sled,
For little dreamers, still in bed.

At the center, a tree of life.
Witness to man's folly and strife,
But also to those lofty ideals,
Each Christmas nurtures and appeals.

Christmas, 1999

– 21 –

TESTAMENTS

A testament of God's power
Beyond the emotion and the fear
Is the real beauty of a flower
Returning, blooming, every year.
And the majestic trees that tower
Protecting the birds that we hear.

I know the sounds of God's presence
In the sereneness of the night
Plus, temples of magnificence
Built to catch a heavenly light.
And the pillars of omniscience
To the glory of divine might.

Yet I feel warmth from God's caring
Deep in the darkness of my soul.
I walk with a regal bearing
A homeless nomad is my role.
Rescued by a feat of daring,
The gift of Jesus makes me whole.

Christmas, 1999

– 22 –

TWO THOUSAND YEARS

Now that we have two thousand years,
Since that true unfathomed birth,
Beyond hopes and happy tears,
A Godly gist to human worth.

As man he was awash in strife,
Yet showed all a different course.
By his glorious mysterious life,
Changed the concept of strength and force.

Over the centuries many have tried
To know, to worship, love and adore.
Creative beauty sanctified.
Sculpture, paintings, words and more,
Churches and spires reach the sky.
Loves uplifting that dignify.

Christmas, 2000

– 23 –

SANTA'S TRAVELS

Rich red velvet coat, flowing gray,
A warm heart in a rotund weigh.
A bottomless sack burdens the sleigh
For children here and a world away.
In just one night of spreading joys,
Sparkles the dreams of girls and boys.

The blowing snow, the tinkling bells,
This touching night the story tells,
Deer that tread on your roof and mine,
In that fleeting second define,
A magic glowing that surrounds,
Those young dreamers, asleep, spellbound.
This spirit of giving and caring,
Lightens the pain many are bearing.

Christmas, 2000

– 24 –

GLORIOUS TREE

Aurora bathes this Holy night,
Golden shafts caresses the tree,
Swirling magic of dancing light,
This is the time for hearts made free.

Imagining in this mosaic glow,
Swaying red and gold balls and lights,
Glimpse the snowman; the grazing doe.
Teddy and titmouse, child's delights,

Snowbirds and bluebirds perambulate,
And I see Santa, reindeer and sleigh,
A Joseph and Mary anxious in wait,
A gold angel above, crowns the way.

Within your mind's eye, can you now see
Are more treasures hidden in this tree?

Christmas, 2001

– 25 –

CHRISTMAS TIME IN NEW YORK CITY

The happy skaters in Central Park,
Neon motion makes light from the dark.
Hear the murmur of the traffic's flight,
Shoppers cast silhouettes in the night.
Decorative lights are everywhere.
Horse drawn carriages are here and there.
The snow hardly falls, it's weight so slight,
The hazy twinkling of high rise lights.
The cold penetrates without pity,
It's Christmas time in New York City.

Christmas, 2002

– 26 –

A LAND of ST. NIKOLAS

A wintry blast off artic steppes,
Deepening nights and swirling snow.
Festive colored lights, twinkling;
Populace, fur clad, on the go.

And now the trees bent and blowing,
Long darkness; the sky a glowing.
Surreal display with dancing light.
Time of peace; if just for tonight.

This land of cupolas and spires.
Of bearded priests, in gold adorned.
Capella, the only sound.
Homage and praise, in Mass is found.

Three generations, empty and low,
Godlessness and nowhere to go.
St. Nikolas; gifts to bestow.
Hearts sustain a spiritual glow.

In this, the harshest of seasons,
Ageless story of hope beyond reason.
People now can worship freely,
The Holy Babe that altered history.

Christmas, 2004

– 27 –

ENCHANTED EVENING

The stars sparkle and the moon's hue,
Reflect on the snow like deepened blue,
The evergreens, each rich full bough,
Ablaze in lights, I know not how.

Many thoughts and dreams abound
Of other nights and magic sound,
When multitudes lived in doubt
Of how existence would turn out.

There was a birth in the deep lonely cold,
The story spread was surprisingly bold,
Striking in content to the prophet's word
Many were heartened with what they now heard.

The lowliest were visited at night.
Kings from the East chased a bright light,
And a dream required a hurried flight.
God, so subtly, showing his might.

To this day with all that we know,
Deep, dark winter has a special glow.
That birth, that life, and all that changed,
Human meaning was now rearranged.

Christmas, 2005

– 28 –

TRINITY CHURCH

The wind blown snow falls on the city,
Flags ripple and the air is gritty.
Deep winter night in canyons of steel,
Streets are quiet, a biting cold feel.
Trinity steeple in grand repose,
Mystical strength, a deep aura glows.

A different scene; a sunny morn.
Sirens wail, and screams of the forlorn,
A September day, so filled with hope,
Then blasts and fire of cosmic scope.
Then the rumble, the roar, the thunder,
Of a tsunami wall of wonder.
This church rushes to comfort and soothe;
Responders who save, or lives they lose.
From horror, uncomprehending grief.
In this refuge, moments of relief.

The canyon walls mask the city's din,
Familiar hymns are raised deep within,
The candles flicker, a warming glow;
Outside is the swirling drifting snow.
Its Christmas Eve and voices are raised,
Sincere hopes for peace and joy be praised.

Christmas, 2006

– 29 –

A DISTANT EVE

Quiet frost in a silver coat,
Barren tree limbs crowding the park.
Boarded fountains, upended boats
Pigeons coo in the mounting dark.

Castle hulks on a nearby hill,
Dream symbol of an ancient past.
The warm lights of the village fill
The hearts of the living crèche cast.

Cold starless eve, crowded whispers
As carolers mark their places,
To begin the Christmas vespers,
Clouds release gentle white traces.

Christmas, 2007

– 30 –

TRANSFORMATION

Its deep rich green and so nicely full,
Ramrod straight and its seven feet tall.
Shake off the snow and in from the cold;
Tiny white lights encircle the boughs.
Untie boxes discolored with age,
To reveal treasures deep in the past;
All shapes, all sizes, each with a tale,
Positioned with an artistic care.
Ribboned to hold each firm to a limb,
Step back, for sight with an approving eye.
And when the fullness is perfection,
Gabriel oversees the top.
Add candy striped canes and popcorn rope.
Then relax by the roaring fire and hope.
A prayer once more for peace and joy,
Symbolic birth of one tiny boy.

Christmas, 2008

– 31 –

STILLNESS

There is a stillness on this night of nights
Flakes are drifting from a steel leaden sky,
Coating trees and roads and distant heights,
As happy souls prepare, and spirits fly,
It's Christmas time; brimming with colored lights
And each child's anticipation is high.
Church bells, old carols, and other delights
The time for our enlightenment is nigh.
For celebrating new life with old sights
Pleas for peace, new faith, and hope, in each sigh.

Christmas, 2009

– 32 –

WHIMSY

I guess it all began with Santa Claus.
This whimsy of spirit Christmas begot,
A generous, chubby giver of gifts,
Who in one night bestows all the world,
With what each has as their fervent desire,
For kids, toys; others, needs; for some hope.

The story has grown and grown over time,
With elves to give aid, and a polar home.
Why there's even a Mrs. Santa Claus,
And magic reindeer, which, by the way, fly.
Lately being led by a red nosed guy,
There is this mystical speed that allows,
The whole world to be gifted in one night.
But no mind; it happens at the speed of light.

Many new adornments have grown, you see.
There's Toyland; pixie Angels, green trees.
Lights of all kinds that twinkle with color.
Some are snowflakes, others tiny like stars.
Empty stocking hung by the hearth with care,
In hopes that by morning, gifts will be there.
Bright colored packages adorn the floor
About a glistened tree with an angel cap.
All of this fluff to remind us of One,
That mankind was given, long, long, ago.

Christmas, 2009

– 33 –

A CHRISTMAS SCENE

Trudge through the narrow and winding street,
To the central square where people meet,
The damp coldness fills the shortened day,
As shoppers melt by, each their own way.

Distant steeple towers scrape the sky.
As low lying clouds are drifting by,
And wisps of snow lightly touch my cheek.
I search for markets and toys I seek.

The trees of green are turning slowly white,
And the fading dusk turns to light night.
To home and warmth on this special eve,
Sharing feast to cherish and receive.

To bed and you cannot help but think,
A new remembrance is on the brink,
Of the birth that scrambled each Man's view,
Showing the truth of God's love anew.

Christmas - 2011

– 34 –

ST. MATTHEW

The ancient prophesies one by one,
Foretold the sequence that's now begun,
Mary with child by Heavenly host,
Joseph's dream filled by the Holy Ghost.
Told to take Mary to be his wife.
She's the vessel for a special life;
And so Jesus was Bethlehem born,
On a chilly early winter morn.

Wise men seeking him came from the East,
Herod, troubled, called the Chief Priest,
Heard a new Prince would come to lead.
Sent off the Kings to fulfill their need.
The newborn rested under the star;
Gave worshipful gifts brought from afar.
Being warned to go another way,
Thwarting Herod's desire to slay.

Christmas, 2011

– 35 –

ST. LUKE

Caesar sent out a census decree,
Each had to go to their own city.
Mary and Joseph had travelled too,
She with a child that soon would be due.
In Bethlehem where the time was right,
For a Holy Birth; a dark cold night.
Wrapped in swaddling; in a manger lay,
Amid God's creatures, and warming hay.

In nearby fields, shepherds watch their flock,
An angel appeared, causing fear and shock.
But the angel brought tidings of joy,
In the city of David; a boy,
A savior for all, this day is born.
And the shepherds went to see this morn.
Worshipped the Babe, in the humble scene,
And spread the word of what they had seen.

Christmas, 2011

– 36 –

THIS CHRIST

This Christ, this miracle.
This birth, this life;
This story, enduring.
Its love; its hope.
It's a guide, Its beyond
More than a life. Eternity.
Monotheistic, breaks the past.
Surmounts man's weakness;
I believe because it speaks to me.
Full freedom to worship as I see.
Not from force or enmity;
Coercing belief on a cowering Me.
Makes your "truth" nothing but heresy.

Christmas, 2012

– 37 –

THIS SANTA CLAUS THING

Sometimes I ponder in the night,
Logistics of a magical sight.
How confusing it must really be,
Many Santas' in stores and TV,
And the story told to girls and boys,
That one flying sleigh delivers toys.

While the tale defies credulity,
A complex structure builds verity.
First, there is the place; the far North Pole.
Filled with Elves that have a major role.
So far away and unseen by all,
Out of consciousness until late fall.

Suddenly anticipation grows.
For sure he'll bring it; everyone knows.
So if you are much older than nine,
Suspend logic, it will all be fine.
A chubby bearded man, dressed in red,
With eight reindeer and a flying sled.
Travels the world when night is stilled;
Gifts beneath trees and stockings filled.

Christmas, 2012

– 38 –

THEN AND NOW

Under winter ice a flowing creek,
Heavy dark clouds foretelling what's bleak,
The town's roofs emitting chimney smoke,
The daylight drifting towards a dusky cloak,
And our flag in a windblown unfurl.
Quiet streets with only leaves a swirl.

And in the square stands a festooned tree,
Heralds the day that's about to be,
A park surrounds and the fountains flow,
With strings of lights and colors aglow,
A cold drizzly rain has turned to snow,
Quietly folks are shopping below,
With lots of bags and children in tow.

It's like a vignette from times long past,
While today's pace is in stark contrast.
In each of us resides, hopes and dreams,
And children's wide eyes are still agleam.
With a vision of a laden sleigh,
From a mystical land far away,
Where angels and fairies dance and play,
Builds morning magic for Christmas Day.

Christmas, 2013

– 39 –

A SPECIAL CHRISTMAS EVE

Christmas Eve, so cold and so crisp,
Clouds and wind, and flakes; just a wisp.
Dinner long done, tree alive and lit,
We pile in the car, a real tight fit.

The church tonight, alive and aglow,
Crowding all seats, filling each row.
Assembly of murmurs, quickly ends,
Lights brighten; the organ ascends.
The entering choir joyfully sings,
A well known carol, like on Angel wings.
Scriptures are all in Bethlehem set,
Recounting the prophecies, all were met.
And as the service is in full swing;
I see that now the choir will sing,
My Poem, set to music, an unknown treat.
Choir stands to the organ's first beat.

Christ, Mary, Joseph

My dear Christ, savoir unborn,
Sweet Mary, Virgin serene,
O' Joseph, so strong, yet scared.
To this mystic unknown, by faith directed.
Angels and Dreams and events unexpected.

My dear Christ, tiny and bare,
Sweet Mary, with tender care.
O' Joseph, grateful in prayer.
Far from Bethlehem's streets, and human jumble;
God's gift of love in a manger so humble.

(continued)

A SPECIAL CHRISTMAS EVE (continued)

My Christmas gift, as tears overflow,
The service ending, my being aglow.
The trip home, like soaring on wings.
Never forgotten, my heart still sings.

Christmas, 2014

– 40 –

UNSEEN --- BUT............

In this vast cosmos where we are,
Millions of light years stretch afar,
Galaxies and stars by Billions;
Vastness still beyond all our minds.

Yet in a tiny speck of dust;
Unseen in the grandest of schemes.
Minds begat a creator idea;
That all of unknown had a plan.
In the evolution of time,
Some sense, some reason, and some rhyme.
For each life there is a purpose,
That may be only known by God.
And refined that this creator,
Cared for those on this speck;
And sent our very own life form.
One to redeem our existence.

I know that it may blow the mind,
With what our eyes now can see.
Is it a possibility?
We may find another life form,
Who also searched for eternity.

Christmas, 2015

Poems from Travels

– 1 –

JOURNEY

The colors of the winter sky,
Deep crimson, burnt orange, dark blue,
This late day beauty brings a sigh.
A peek of God's creation; a tiny view.

Darkness descends, shadows appear,
Sliver moon, feeling of fear,
Ground fog is thick, hiding the trees,
The stillness chokes, there is no breeze.

How fast from brightness to the deep,
Just as life, from joy to weep,
But in the cold, some strength I'll find,
I must be bold. I steel my mind.

I walk in darkness and yet know,
My inner light will surely glow.
In able hands, this life I trust,
My God is love, is peace, is just.

Christmas, 2003

– 2 –

PARISIAN SPRING

The Queen of cities in sunny Spring,
Is each and everything,
Written, said, wished, or sung.
She touches a universal chord
That exhilarates the soul.

Our windowed room looks over,
Winding streets of stonier gray.
The trees, their buds prepared,
Early blooms dot balconies.
Up along the boulevard,
Sidewalk tables start to fill,
Drinking café or wine with lips,
Eying girls with furtive sips.

Days filled going sight to sight.
From Arch to Louvre to Eiffel Tour;
Notre Dame, L'Opera, and Tombs,
Tuilleries, Obelisk, Sacre Coeur.
Awe in the great detail,
Such beauty on a grand scale.

Immersing too, the feeling side,
Narrow, naughty, Montparnesse.
Freeing air of Left Bank tide,
And twisting through it all.
Rippled silver flowing Seine,
So many bridges span it,
Thousand boats glide in it.

(continued)

Parisian Spring (continued)

As the still, cool, dusk fades.
Night lights in unison appear.
Life renews and in high gear,
Lido, Folies, and Moulin Rouge.
Dashing cabs and subway, too.
Fatigued city rests for one short hour
Just as dawn's beams overpower.

November 12, 1974

– 3 –

ONE ALPINE NIGHT

The Bernese Oberland astounds,
Interlaken by Alpine walls,
A valley womb where peaks surround
Lauterbrunnen, overnight call.

Finishing dinner of rabbit and veal,
A village stroll – almost unreal.
Moon enlivens the crusty snow,
Big bright stars hang ever so low.

Soundless, but for our crunching feet
On rolling, darkened, lifeless streets;
Rising straight in endless sheer.
Infamous Eiger – that climbers fear.
Image and feel, still this day so clear.

March 18, 1975
(At the foot of Eiger Alp in Switzerland)

– 4 –

GLIMPSES OF SWISS

A full of glee winter fantasy,
A tiny land of sky high snow,
Exploring rugged Swiss diversity,
An inner dream; glowing dignity.

From Basel's gay Carnivale tone,
Costumed revelers and pastry shops,
To the south; from the valley floor,
Leaping Alpine peaks stunningly soar,

Medieval treasure; the city of Bern,
Arcades, towers; ornate, complex clocks
The burg astride ridges and hills.
While fountains are hidden and boxed.

A hillside rest in Montreux Lodge.
Ice skating by Lac Leman shores
Sole movement one could scarcely see,
A summer resort, now people free.

A morning tour of Castle Chillon,
Made so famous in Byron's poem.
Soon the traces of graceful Geneve,
A finished pearl on far lake shore.

Patterns so repeated from town to town,
Nights spent buried in thick goose down,
Touch icy dawn floor and quickly awoke,
Hearty breakfast acts as a furnace stoke.

(continued)

GLIMPSES OF SWISS (continued)

Now the trip takes a northward track,
Toward Luzern, brings bustling back,
Deep clouds shield Mt. Pilatus from view,
The lake reflects gray, and I am too.

Leaving the swans at municipal pier,
Head to Zurich as the sun reappears.
Imposing Cathedral and statues too,
Meandering ways, laden shoppes to view.

Lake Constance teems, like a holiday.
Hordes walk and skate, plus horse drawn sleighs.
Now headed home with mixed emotion,
To return once more a fast growing notion.

April 8, 1975

– 5 –

CHRISTMAS IN FRANKFURT

The icy chilling northern wind,
Sweeps off the Taunus slopes,
Heralding the Advent days.
Twinkling white bathes city blocks,
Over human mass in disarray
Sparkling panes reflect red and green
Coaxing glances and beckon in.

Freshly brewed “Weinnachtbock”
Konditori cases, stollen show,
Pfeffernuse and gelb also.
It’s St. Nickolas, the young await.
Where began “O Tannenbaum”
And Grebers’ “Silent Night.”
On Christmas Eve, stillness comes,
All homes aglow, on empty streets.
Ovens roast the tender goose,
Family at hand, breathes inward warmth.

Candled spire, chimes a midnight song,
Carols and chorus pierce the dark
“Stillige Nacht” casts a spell of awe,
And from communions feeling glow,
To snowy crisp and bathing moon
Whispered eye nod and peaceful touch.

Christmas, 1975

– 6 –

BUDAPEST IMAGES

THE DREAM

Through a balcony's windowed view,
Heavy boiling. Rolling puffs of gray
Crosscut the hills of lush thick green;
Steep slopes meet the wide Danube flow.
A chilliness permeates the air,
Dull buildings dominate everywhere.
From the warmth of the inside I go,
To walk alone crowded streets below.
Where mingling soldiers dominate.
Suddenly, some fear creeps upon me.
My dream retreats to the balcony,
Turning a back on this Buda view.
Tread the large window paneled room.
Gazing upon the opposite sight,
A rolling green lea bathed in light;
Falling away in deep hilly flight.
People picnicking and strolling paths.
Their goal a distant amusement park,
With Ferris wheel and gala fun things,
Whiff! – All images gone from my mind.

(continued)

– 7 –

BUDAPEST IMAGES
THE REALITY

On Fisherman's Bastion parapet
Above the swollen Danube's flow.
Wild, wide, muddy, picturesque.
Almost skimming the bridges and banks.
Below a sky of hazy pale blue.
Sun's warmth refreshes; breezes cool;
River twists, turns, snakes its way,
Old city clashes with high-rise new.
Beauty and life together are seen.
Walking crowded streets, vibrant and gay.
The people seem the same as we.
Hilly Buda, on to supine Pest.
Full of sights as time unfolds,
From Parliament to Palace walls,
Margaret's Island and Heroes Square.
Zoo and parks; a lake load of boats.
Carnival rides and divertissement.

After both the dream and real are done,
A strange blend of two psyches, not one.

April 23, 1976

– 8 –

CAFÉ STARK – 1955

Store front shop on cobbled street;
Corner entrance, jingling bell,
Marble chip floor always scrubbed.
Cases groan with fresh baked treats,
And tucked behind, a larger room,
Where meals are lovingly prepared.
Served on marble topped tables,
With comfortable cane backed chairs.
Food for kings at paupers' rates.
Cabbage, salad, schnitzel, or steak.
Wine, coffee, and strudel; everything great.
All the unspoiled atmosphere,
Those friendly diners hold most dear.

CAFÉ STARK – 1975

The setting was much the same.
Trolleys and traffic choked the front.
Side still lined with big shade trees.
The entrance was just the same,
But the jingling bell was gone.
Newer cases displayed the wares,
As succulent as yester years.
It was the back room that changed.
Now paneled with rugs and drapes.
Formal wooden tables and chairs.
The menu was the shock.
Pastry, tea, snacks and beers.

(continued)

CAFÉ STARK (continued)

Gone, hearty meals of bygone years.
Now only a place for break,
Not robust food for body and soul.
An expectancy gone in a puff!
A lesson has been taught.
Reliving the past goes for naught.

1975 & 1977

– 9 –

POLISH COUNTRY CHRISTMAS

Rationed light of a winter sky.
Heavy clouds spreading gentle flakes
On rolling matted frozen fields.
And the rutted stony roads
Clustered on the valley floor,
Strong homes, some with barns along.
In the central square, the well.
Also the church, with golden dome,
Where the cooling drink of God is found.
And time flows slow and endlessly.

Now the silent dark enveloping shawl
Brings flame to hearth and oil lamp glow.
Then the bell peals a festive call
To gather within those fieldstone walls
To sing – and rehear the Savior's birth.
In silence they now fill the square.
Candles flicker in the cold night air.
Crunching feet and voices raised
In carols; passing from home to home.
And a simple loving joy thus spread
Sends frozen tears over weathered cheeks.

Through light warm doorways within,
Glowing coals layer rough stone hearths,
Kettles steamy aroma fills each home.
Straw is spread throughout the floor.
Modeling the ancient stable, this night.
Drawing remembrance of the Holy Child.
Whose primitive birth bathed Earth with light.

(continued)

POLISH COUNTRY CHRISTMAS (continued)

Women and girls active, preparing the feast.
Men and boys nearby, dress the tree,
Soon, all gather for the symbolic meal.
Twelve courses, disciples, tribes.
No serving of flesh. Borscht begins;
Cold salad, three varieties of dumplings.
Cabbage precede, carp, perch, and cod.
And now a hearty pudding; Kutia.
Two different fruits, round the repast.
A tradition complete, the image enhanced.
Expectancy quickly fills the air,
Exchange of gift with a happy glow.
Then all asleep; dream images flow
The spirit is nourished; seeds left to grow.

Christmas, 1977

(special thanks to Rev. Adam Kucma of Warsaw, Poland.
[long deceased]
His sharing from life made this possible,)

– 10 –

REFLECTION

Christmas Eve: darkness has fallen.
And the chill bites your very bones;
Lights reflect from cobbles and tracks,
And a misty snow, lightly blown.
Measured steps of a lonely man,
On barren streets with gifts in hand.
Casting glances at home on home,
Where inside resides warm lit glows.
Savory smoke and songs of joy,
Ignore the figure passing by.
Much like the folk of Bethlehem,
Nineteen eighty-one years ago.

Christmas, 1981

– 11 –

GRACHEN
(SWITZERLAND)

Perched high above a white puff sea,
This gently sloping Alpine lea,
The steep sheer rock the road entwines
Transports you to a state of mind.

Distant hamlets so tiny now
Sounds of bells, on each grazing cow.
Always, always, the sound of bells,
Soothing the heart; casting their spells.

Waning moon in a hazy light,
The biting coolness of the night,
The meadow paths, the curling smoke.
Church bells that mark the quarter stroke.

The smells, the food, the muffled cheer,
The warmth of hoisted steins of beer,
The feel, unseen, of towering peaks,
Luring clouds, like 'hide and seek.'

The early morning sounds of life,
Children; baker; a farmers' wife,
Golden rays set the peaks aglow,
Reflect the swirling windblown snow.

September, 1987

– 12 –

SNIPS OF SCOTLAND

Endless dots on rust filled fields,
Grazing woolen gray and browns,
Treeless valleys and rock strewn slopes,
Shafts of sun, while clouds are dumping.
Lakes and hills with unremitting winds,
Sails are bending.
Whitecaps blending.

Beyond the reach of Hadrian's' wall
Dwells a fierce, friendly folk,
Of legend and sad history.
Across the dells and tors and moors,
Hear the bagpipes mournful sound,
And the presence of the sea all around.

Heather in blue and red and yellow,
Bathe the low mountainsides.
Little stone houses huddle in warmth.
Square green common, a single spire,
Narrow straight streets, like fabric weave.

Mists and clouds hugging the hills,
Long black lakes are foreboding.
A single boat transgresses.
Intermittent rocks and ruins,
Creating an expectant air,
That breeds myths of a monster lair.

(continued)

SNIPS OF SCOTLAND (continued)

Villages of tight built stone,
And aged rocky lines;
Climbing, crossing as a huge jigsaw,
Set in order, long, long ago.
And castle ruins remind,
That the ages are always near
Of many violent battles fought here;
Where Scot and English shed their blood.
While forging their tenuous history.

The Royal city shaped by the sea,
And the ancient fortress rock and walls.
A center vibrant with intensity,
Grand scale, stately, with old world charm.

These are a few selected snips,
A "wee dram" no more than a sip.

Christmas, 1991

– 13 –

DECEMBER IN MANHATTAN

A biting north wind is channeling through,
Vertical canyons of steel, stone, and glass.
Swirling crystal flecks dust the avenue.
Horns and whistles, Santa bells and cold brass,
Muffled hum of humanity packed tight,
It's a Manhattan pre-holiday sight.

All ages of children caught in the flow,
Bundled excitement, fantasy windows.
A smell of chestnuts from hundreds of carts,
While horse drawn carriages vie for a part
Of streets filled with buses, limos, and cabs,
Each looking for an advantage to grab.

Thousands of colors fill a tree like spice,
Five deep to glimpse the skaters on ice.
Bright colored bags flowing over with gifts,
And the mind hears music drifting like mist.
Neon fashions whimsical night like day
Where throngs, after dinner, wander to plays.

Finally; some quiet soothes over all,
The wind dies down, heavy snowflakes fall.
Late at night with the energy faded,
Scramble against cold, for warmth is traded.

Christmas, 1992

– 14 –

SEDONA

High sky of unbending blue,
Pinnacles and cliffs from ages made.
Constant heat beats the dusty floor.
Reflecting a shimmering mirage
Time seems locked between now and when.
The parade of seasons is now and then,
Gone. And the cycle revolves again.
Man has made his tracks herein.
Drawn by sight, held by soul,
Created beauty, inevitably scarred,
Unable to leave or let go.
In tension – the timeless and
The undiscovered psyche.

Christmas, 1993

– *15* –

EVENSONG
(VESPERS)

The daily toiling course is run,
And bending rays of late day sun,
Reflect on vaulted strength of stone,
And softness of the stained glass shown.

Children in starched red are scurrying;
Worshippers from their jobs are hurrying.
Mounted bells announce the “Evensong”,
To praise the day, or right a wrong.

Hymns of thanks in pipes and voice,
Each day, some way, worthy rejoice.
The past, the night; new dawn to be,
To future, hope, expectancy.

Refrain

And now I pray at setting sun,
That God has blessed this day now run.
As I look toward the growing night,
Keep me closely in your sight.
Open me to your loving way,
To grow and cherish each new day.

Another Refrain

This life is given for us to use,
This creation not meant to abuse.
Can we pull our souls from the fire?
Will enough of your children still aspire,
To save this Island we all share,
From the darkness of human despair.

April, 1993

– 16 –

TIME WALK

The woods and lakes, these rippled hills,
Manicured, level and pat,
Jumbled sounds from everywhere.
Off walls that mock the time.
Drawn to that which was.
Lets imagination stay free,
And dream the sounds of history.

Warm and wet and misty fog,
Deliberate procession moving,
Carriages and stallions sound,
Piercing the early dawn stillness.
Lords, Ladies, and those awaiting,
To Fountains for Yule celebrating.

Padres and those who believe,
On a mission to conceive,
Their own retreat to The God.
Drawn to this wild land,
Escaping from worldly sin.
To build outwardly and in.

The Legions on a forced march,
Tread these forests and leas.
Reinforcing Hadrian's Wall,
Far limit of the Empire,
Keeping the darkness out,
Two millennium ago.

Fall. 1994

(Fountains Hall in Northern England, near York, was built as a Cistercian Monastery in 1132. In 1610 it was rebuilt from ruins. It now lies in ruins again.)

– 17 –

SUNSET AT VICTORIA HARBOR

Quietly at the water's edge.
Soaking the senses and feelings,
Gentle breezes whisk our faces.

The sun sinks lower in the sky,
Waves in disarray, lap the piles,
The hazy shade, the golden rays,
Their patterns reflect pulsing life.
Rising tall from the island shore,
Graceful stone and steel wrapped facades,
And the steep rise of sweeping slopes,
Mosaic backdrop for it all.

Now just a glow above the hills,
The water has turned deep purple,
Sailing junks seek their home,
Ships horns warn of the coming dark,
And a twinkling of lights appear,
One by one, the high rises glow,
Then; an explosive neon flow.
The show complete, a night alive,
Sight, sounds; Hong Kong floods the mind.

Christmas, 1995

– 18 –

CITY BY THE BAY

The bay is bathed in bright moonlight,
Twinkling dots on the distant shore,
Hints of fog in fading twilight,
My heart explores above the core.

Teeming cable cars strain on hills,
And wind filled flags bend each pole.
The vibrant life. The dusk air chills.
I am a part; a piece of His whole.

Extending towards a sunset view,
Sausalito and Golden Gate,
Sky ablaze with a rosy hue,
Silhouettes a ship, also my fate.

Christmas, 1997

– 19 –

AUGUST LAKE LOUISE

A boathouse, desolate, reflected,
A lake laps at craggy rock walls.
Driven flakes in the fading light.
Dark black green of clustered trees,
Tingling with the heavy flaked snow.
Crystal air and hanging clouds,
Encrusted delphinium blue.
Flights of robins in a muddled maze,
Flags are stiffly straight.
The mountain saddle beyond the rising mist,
Cradling glaciers well-worn ice.

From the warmth inside the stately hall,
Of Chateau Lake Louise.
The diners seem barely aware,
Engrossed in a gentle hum,
With music made for reverie
Filling the mind and tweaking the soul;
Transports me to a world apart,
Of sense, sound, and towering mind art.

August, 2001

– 20 –

OUR TOWERS

The golden sun falls on the far Jersey hills,
Windy ripples on the fresh Hudson tide,
Light puffy clouds drawn on a string,
Bright amber lights and the city revives,
In this glass and steel cocoon on high,
We drink and dine while touching the sky.

Then on a clear, serene September morn,
The power of Satan from out of the deep,
Rained pure hatred and killed innocence,
Terror and death and all did weep,
Fires of hell and the towers collapse,
Dust and smoke filled the holes in our heart.

A wellspring of caring and courage was tapped.
Heroes and leaders, once maligned were reborn.
And we were many; yet were also one.
So this battle with evil is now fully joined,
Through thunder, fire, siege, and stealth,
Fulfilling a longing to be peaceful and free.

Christmas, 2001

– 21 –

THE BEACHES

Imagine an armada, sheathed in stealth,
Eerie silence, a moonless night.
Thousands of boats wrap the horizon,
Quiet cold steel and flesh for now,
The droning din, clouds filled with planes,
Staccato of guns, flash the fog.

Suddenly all hell is unleashed,
Among these sandy dunes and beach,
Waves and waves of humanity
Thrusting themselves upon the shore;
To penetrate this fortress wall,
With freedom and light as the goal.
And much suffering lies ahead,
Until the evil Axis is dead.

Three score summers have come and gone,
The low clouds spit, the sands lie cold.
Trotters train near the water line,
Some rusted steel, all that remains.

And I walk these hallowed beaches,
Taking photos, retrieving sand.
Among bunker relics left to stand.
From this epic now so long ago
Where brave young men gave it all,
Knowing what they had to do.
Freedom at stake for me and you.
Let's not forget their sacrifice
Let's not profane their fondest hopes.

(continued)

THE BEACHES (continued)

Above Omaha, on Sacred ground
A quietness of peace is found.
In rows of white crosses and stars,
Ten thousand lie at rest right here.
Feelings overwhelm, eyes flood with tears.

Will mankind never seem to learn?
Even though peace is what we yearn
The forces of chaos are ever so strong
The human continuum muddles along.

Summer, 2003

– 22 –

LE BATEAUX DE PARIS

Radiant brightness is sinking,
Makes marble glow; sets glass aflame.
A gentle splash, a rocking groan.
Led to a table, two alone.
Clink of glass, bubbles on lips,
Gazing as city lights twinkle,
Shades of salmon on wispy clouds;
And the noise of many, just a hum.
Restraining, ropes are cast ashore,
And now the magic ride begins.

Amidships band strikes an upbeat tune;
In silence and slowness, we move;
Dancing lights beneath each bridge.
Marble structures reflect a glorious past.
And time seems suspended in mist.
A harvest moon slowly rising,
Our wine flows, its fruited scent;
We dine and partake as a feast.

On rutted, time worn stone paths
Families find the evening to play,
And lovers really stroll the banks,
While some just snuggle and hold tight.

Ile de Cite and Notre Dame,
Bathed in soft and shadowy light.
The strains of ‘Ave Maria’ intone.
We pause to now, digest it all.

(continued)

LE BATEAUX DE PARIS (continued)

Talk of images that stretch the mind,
A dream quality surrounds it all.
And when, too soon, it's at an end,
Monsieur Eiffel's Tour comes alive.
It's a Grand Finale, light show.
Silently we ride to our abode,
While etching sights, feelings, and sounds.

Christmas, 2004

– 23 –

A RUSSIAN ENCOUNTER

On a strange street and somewhat lost,
A gypsy child yells "Hey" to me.
Big brown eyes and dirty hands,
Unkempt dress and well-worn shoes.

She runs and points where I should go,
Then extends her palm for a coin.
I look for coins and I have none.
I say "ssssh" and give her a large bill.
Her eyes grow wide and she runs to tell
Of her gift. Yet my gift is many fold.

Christmas, 2004

(Actual happening in St. Petersburg, Russia)

– 24 –

THE DANUBE

The sea shimmers to the horizon reach
And laps gently on the sandy beach.
Early Tribes and Greeks were hailed,
And Roman Legions marched and sailed.

This mighty river so steeped in lore,
Brought pain and joy and lots of war.
Where Roman lords and Bulgari kings,
Wielded power that conquest brings.

Yet these vibrant shores attracted
Traders who thrived and interacted.
From East and West, exotic goods
And towns were born out of the woods.

Forts protected both farms and trade;
Cities grew and riches were made.
The Christian faith spread to the east.
Sees, monasteries, and local priests.

Nations grew, boundaries defined.
Power and intrigue was not confined.
Cross and crescent battled it out,
At times who prevailed cast in doubt.

From the Alpine's deep snowy store,
To the Black Sea's delta shore,
The twists and turns that ages have made,
Ebb and flow and flood cascades.

(continued)

THE DANUBE (continued)

Danube, Donau, in folk songs and lore,
For eons piercing at Europe's core.
Weaving a uniqueness of mystery,
From the mistiness of history.

Christmas, 2005

– 25 –

SANTORINI

Early summer mornings misty haze,
Accent the sunrises golden rays,
The blue Aegean churns in our wake,
Filled from the void of an ancient quake.
Walls of black, and lava brown-red
This steep and crescent isle; dead ahead.

On the craggy, stony, sun baked spines,
Filled with windswept trees and crawling vines.
Myriad Chapels with deep blue domes,
Pastels and whites, steep cliff hanging homes.
And as the sun now rolls from its high,
With those puffy clouds dotting the sky,
Lattice laden greens, flowers of white,
Pots blooming red; an eye soothing sight.
Walking undulating steps and streets
Witness smells and sounds very Greek.
Resting spot on a cliff hanging deck.

And when the late sun has gone to rest,
Coming to life on the Island crest,
Sparkling air and twinkling light
Creating a sight as we take flight.
It's now blazoned, imagining my mind.
Panoramic, as an unworldly find.

Christmas, 2006

– 26 –

HOURS BEFORE SUNRISE

It's four AM in the summer heat,
Rolling through the cobbled streets,
Eternal city of ancient sites.
Bathed in soft illumined lights.
Sidewalks and plazas fast asleep;
Full moon casts shadows deep.
A couple of ladies of the night
In lonely pursuit before daylight.

And the psyche wanders this night,
In the whirr of this speeding flight;
To ancient days of the Roman might.
This city ruled its world through fright.
The Forum was in its glory.
But each dweller had to worry,
About surviving through the night.
For pagan Rome was in a fight.
These hills and ruins, like a dream,
Tell of harshness; a primal scream.
Life's cheap within Roman power,
Dimming the cultural flower.

And Christians were forced to beware.
Their faith was tested everywhere.
The catacombs, a secret lair.
Lest they be Coliseum fare.

Abruptly back to now I'm drawn,
As streaks of sunlight, signal dawn.
Our trip now over; heading home.
From the truth that is modern Rome.

Summer, 2007

– 27 –

A MUMBAI DAY
(March, 2008)

This restful cove on the Arabian Sea
Eons of Greeks, Buddhists, Hindus too
Portuguese next and the Brits for tea,
From this a port and city grew.
Colonial rule and finally free,
Complex, diverse, an Indian glue.

Our ship serenaded by a red clad band,
Morning sun casts an ecru haze,
From the trains at the start of days,
Millions on foot in full command
Vehicles navigate this human maze,
To work; in rote as an unseen hand.

Contrasts abound with every view
Lush apartments surround the bay,
And squalor and begging a turn away,
Sights of temples from the colonial day
And high rise glass, the modern pulse,
The city remains alive at night
'Queens' Necklace' provides circular light;
Carriage rides and nightlife abound,
India's new vibrancy astound.

(continued)
==================================

A MUMBAI DAY (continued)

(November, 2008)

Imagine the horror and the grief,
A terror attack beyond belief.
The chaos, the fear beyond despair,
Sucking the life right out of the air.

Fall, 2008

(We visited Mumbai eight months before
the terror attack in November.)

– 28 –

TAORMINA

A bus climbs a steep and winding trail,
Sheer cliff walls and no protective rail,
The Ionian Sea spreads below,
And the distant Etna's smoking glow.
I am disgorged at the ancient gate.
By walled remains meant to isolate;
I begin my walk where Greeks did play,
Long eras before the Christ held sway.

Corso Umberto forms the main street,
People teeming to meet and to greet.
And the buildings that line this way,
Filled with shops and many a café.
Left and upwards; viewing the blue Med sea,
Through cliff hanging homes, flowers and trees.
And suddenly in all noble grace,
A Greek Theatre; tragedies place.

Winding back through the fragrant trees
To Piazza Aprile sunny with breeze.
A crowd awaits the carriage drawn bride,
To the Baroque church in graceful pride.
Today's charm with hillside clinging homes,
With some walls dating to ancient Rome,
For eons man has sought to soothe the soul.
Here meets sky and sea. The beauty is whole.

Christmas, 2011

– 29 –

THE GRAND EXPERIMENT
PART 1

They came to these shores to seek a new life
Persevering, during sickness and strife.
And yet a spirit of “must do” prevailed,
Mere survival against odds this entailed.
In time they grew and made a life of sorts;
Yet distant from Europe’s classes and courts.

They had come with differing views and doubt.
Religious duress had driven them out.
But this new land had been scary and dark.
Adversity and pain had left its mark.
Starting with naught but a survival need.
A warm place, cover, and sustenance feed.

In due time the population had grown,
Towns were created, and governance shown.
The people together would find a consent,
For laws and rules with citizen assent.
There would be a growing need to break out;
A new world is ready to show its clout.

Even afar they were subjects of kings,
And from time to time this caused bullying.
These free men of towering intellects
Became weary of those old world expects.
So they gathered together to agree,
How they would express their need to be free.

(continued)

THE GRAND EXPERIMENT
PART 1
(continued)

Of course this action would make a big fight,
With old Great Britain and all of its might.
Deep forged in the heat of battle and grit;
A flame of freedom forever be lit.
These colonies became United States.
We were now on a road to find our fates.

Christmas, 2012

Poems from the Journey of Life

– 1 –

THE RIVER

The Group, the dark,
The road, the sky,
Hands held, small talk,
The sky, the stars
Illumines the dust and stones
That marks the way.
Time quickly goes.

Then the river,
Churning sounds, and relentless motion.
The mist hangs on the banks.
Upward to bathe the stars
In soft halos of light.

Again the river; endless, endless
We fall silent --- Peace.
This must be it and closeness.
Mountain ridge so dark, so old,
Stately tree on distant bank
Your shape must make you proud.
Twinkles of light tell us
Other humanity, too, is here.

Again the river, endless, endless.
Visions of past happy days.
Laughing children, bright sun,
Warm day, giggling, joy
A cacophony of sound.

(continued)

THE RIVER (continued)

Floating, splashing, sharing.
Swift current, sparkling water,
Dusty road, running, jumping,
Towels and shoes excitedly thrown.
Oh Life! How beautiful!

Again the river, endless, endless,
Fantasies of moods a world away;
Resistance to a Nazi horde,
Meets a U Boat, on a night like this.
Expectancy, stealth, hearts and hopes.
In some small way, we make our mark.
Meaning and purpose in our acts.
Life or death freely mixed.

Again the river, endless, endless,
Renewed, sparked for the moment.
Retrace our journey, deepened.
Floating steps, fear unknown.
Cornfield on the right.
Stalks so straight and tall.
Now the glimmer around the bend.
Home and warmth, outside and in.

October 16, 1971
(First poem I wrote at the Church Retreat House in West Virginia
with a fantasy toward the end)

– 2 –

MAMA BERRY

Recall with pain the early days
When first I was aware of her.
My mind, as such, was infantile.
I was clouded with anxiety.
As Ann's friend, she focused jealousy.
Within me dwelt a gnawing envy.

Outward beauty was not her forte,
A nose oversized upon her face,
And statuesque she never was
Yet to her, God gave abundantly.

Heritage of the tight little Isle,
Verbal flavor to tickle the ear,
Infectious laugh for all to hear,
Stately walk, elegant and clear,
Her eyes, more kind than any made,
Would leave a Queen in the shade.

Slowly the cloud was raised,
As irrational thought removed,
And I could say "Dear Friend."
Love could flow in veins,
Once so cold and closed.

Next came the years of joy,
Often sharing time, we three,
A close, caring intimacy.
She knew so much of life,
Its' lessons, full of adversity,
Only served to deepen her.

(continued)

MAMA BERRY (continued)

Expectations of joy at hand,
When dinner parties had been planned.
Invitations valued and sought,
Schedules scanned so a miss was naught.
For here, diverse personalities,
The lonely, the laudy, some jaded gents,
Yet common in one bond;
Mama Berry knit us all
As in a warming woolen shawl.

All saw in her a friend
She filled a hundred needs.
By giving, she, too, received
Restored a faith to believe.
And when I needed listening,
She was there to hear.

As if a veil came down,
Immortal she was not to be,
Life that coursed very strong
Flowed and ebbed and slowed.
Death came. It could not be
But there it was, unmistakably.

In a chapel bright and warm
A spirit remembered, not gone.
Tears flowed unashamed,
A painful loss was real.
And on a shaded grassy plot
Amid soldiers gone before,
Final rest; soul with her Lord.

(continued)

MAMA BERRY (continued)

Now to her home as often before,
A party with her friends.
The only thread of common tie
She had touched each and everyone;
Her spirit floated up on high.

But I was burdened with my loss,
And when no more could I stay,
I silently turned and walked away.
And as I gently clicked the gate,
Walking that path, pondering the fate.
Knowing that I had shut the door,
To return that way, nevermore.

Mama Berry will always be,
A hallowed, sacred person for me
I gained and grew, much because she
Saw beyond a scared infantile me.

November, 1972

– 3 –

ABOUT THE RAGING FLOW

The rain flow continues in the night,
Then morning grays still leaden light.
A light misty haze hangs over all.
Convert the creek's roaring fall.
A timeless flowing downhill race.
Booms and churns at a frantic pace.
Perched astride a plank foot bridge.
A sagging safe sanctuary,
An immerse thoughts in fantasy.

Rock ledges challenge the water wall.
Patterns smoothed, then broken and barred.
Some inundated and lost for now,
Forcing others to make water part.
Some seem stately in the swirling midst.
Others aloof, yet to be reached.

Dainty blooms safe by torrents cage
Soft green strands overhang the rage.
One boulder can cause a leaping falls,
Some stringy grass stands untouched at all.
Uprooted tree from bygone storms,
A silent, naked, cold gray wall.

The misty haze lifts after all,
And gentle drops cease their fall,
And back from dreams, sunlight calls.

September 11, 1973

– 4 –

THE LAST TOUCHDOWN

A hazy late autumn day,
The closing game at home.
Hope long since flown away.
No way to anticipate
The moment yet to come.

A bench can so lonely be,
For talent that bloomed so long.
Minds are flooded with memories,
Another, thousands have come to see.
But plans reduce the probability
Time and game are flying by.

Now the tumult begins its rise;
The Old General takes the field
The well-known trot, on bowed legs.
Number nineteen on the back.
In glistening white on blue.

Age may have claimed a toll,
Time overtakes us one and all.
Thousands rise for one last cheer.
Can John throw just one more "bomb"?
We hope and plead for just one more.

Two runs leave us six to go,
And third down now is at hand.
Probably a quick down and out;
A first down will keep us going.
And let the bomb come later on.

(continued)

THE LAST TOUCHDOWN (continued)

Yes, for sure it's a pass.
The General scans the scene,
He looks and pumps and throws,
And Hinton snags the seam
Sidesteps a sprawling head and arm,
And accelerates his stride.

Like a cheetah in full flight;
The sidelines blurred by speed,
And sixty thousand on their feet,
A teary ecstasy of screams,
Hinton runs like a demon seen
Crosses the goal – and its no dream.

Up field the hunching Johnny U
Ambles under a splitting din,
And I can guarantee dear friend,
That's a moment I'll always see,
Through tears – the last TD!

December, 1973

(John Unitas is a Hall of Fame quarterback for the Baltimore Colts
who passed away in 2002.
I saw the last TD to Wide Receiver Eddie Hinton.)

– 5 –

THE DINNER GROUP

For most of twenty childhood years
As contemporaries we grew
Pairs wed; embarking on careers.
For close to twenty years more,
In periodic rhythm we dined,
This loose knit group of related peers.

Unpracticed lifestyle, now brand new;
Apartment dwelling was the first.
Informality the brew,
Each gathering enjoyed
Entertaining times were so few.

Soon a second stage began,
With announcements often made,
Of impending birth or births,
One by one, the mothers grew,
Cradled brand new pink and blue.

Apartments too small for cribs and pens,
And production came in a faster rate.
Like we might overpopulate
Then in a flash, it ceased.
Like a secret had been breached.

Over the years many abodes have changed,
From Cambridge on the Eastern Shore,
Silver Spring, Hagerstown and Baltimore.
Through snow, wind, or summer pour,
Six pairs converged; where once were four.

(continued)

THE DINNER GROUP (continued)

The laughs, the talk, the muted hope,
Maybe a respite from mental pain,
Or unexpressed, afraid to share.
Was true support really there?
The shallow times we feared to bare.

There were the games so often played
None more fun than tough charades.
Where the book most often shoved.
'Boxwoods, I have known and loved'.
Where inhibitions found release
Our time each night slipped by like grease.

There were at times family strains
Marriage problems and children pains,
Yet somehow we did not trust enough
And while intuitively aware,
We all pretended they were not there.

Through these impetuous driving years,
Our values sustained abundant change,
New life meanings to many came
In hazy ways some wisdom too.
Maybe life and age teaches you,
Also, the inner being grows
How or why, God only knows.

For most, this life's road is arduous
Stages of life are thrust upon us.
To middle years with kids half grown
Sudden challenges forced to face,
A life in jeopardy, too soon
A marriage torn, turmoil and fear,
We're up to date – Where from here –?

February, 1975

– 6 –

PETS, PETS, PETS

It all began with Hollyberry.
A calico Christmas pussycat,
Who strayed, alas, upon the turf,
Of our close neighbors Siamese.
Losing a silent, violent, scuff,
Disappeared in the winter breeze.

And when we had a new address,
"Free kitten" ads were gently scanned,
Gray striped female did our doorway bless.
In time when our "Tabby" was mature,
Suitors appeared from everywhere.
Tiny squeals in closet here and there.

Now several litters were allowed.
Our friends needs were all supplied.
Held a young male, an angora mix.
Then took Mom to the vet for a fix.
Finally had to give our "Fluffy" away,
"Tabby" again ruled the house, I'd say.

Innocently enter my sister Sue,
With cuddly gerbil, almost brand new.
Now a cage and accouterments,
Kept our cat for hours entranced.
Many close calls; many lonely days,
At last expired in a mysterious way.

(continued)

PETS, PETS, PETS (continued)

Well, some goldfish came from time to time,
Some were bought at the five and dime.
Other won from school "fun fair" game.
In colors and size, no two the same,
Fish bowl soon proved not big enough,
So aquarium equipped, and all that stuff.

More ways to die, you couldn't invent,
Some had trouble with foul water and went,
Others, I think got too close to the top,
And a sharp eyed cat who pawed like a mop.
Heart failure claimed perhaps one or more,
Suicides were often picked off the floor.

With fanfare a brown fluffy pup arrived,
Cuter than anything that man contrived,
This four footed little bundle of joy,
By choice, a female and not a boy.
Spoiled, oh yes! But trained, oh my!
I thought at times we all would cry.

This Sheltie somehow got "Quick" as a name,
She and our cat played an exploring game.
An uneasy truce, that sometimes is broken,
Hisses, whelps, even scratches a token.
A cat's aloofness; then need attention.
Dogs friendliness; I need not mention.

(continued)

PETS, PETS, PETS (conclusion)

And let's not forget the parakeets,
The first with cage, a charity event,
Green, friendly Jasper, a really fine pet,
Flew – playing a game called "Hard to get."
Unafraid to perch on shoulder or head,
Singing and chirping, but no words were said.

Left with neighbors while the family away,
Returned with a feeling, Jasper not okay.
A predawn call to tell, he had died.
Brought home by Jeanne, and all of us cried.
Others have followed. A pretty blue fellow,
And now the basement houses a green and yellow.

Because of Sue, we got a mouse or two,
These pets too, our cat would quietly view.
Safe in a cage, on squeaky treadmill.
"Smokey" and "Snowfur", under a tissue hill.
So often one or another would disappear,
This always accompanied by shedding a tear.

Recent addition, a stray dog named "Benji."
Boggled the mind, while raising energy.
Fights ensued with incumbent dog or cat.
Accidents increased and all like that.
"Benji" went. Quiet back in the Bohnet zoo.
Now numbering, dog, a cat, and parakeets too.

March 4, 1975

– 7 –

THE GULL

The cooling swirling breezes
Mediterranean blue,
White caps and rolling swells
Sorrento's steep cliffs
Your panorama to view.

Graceful white wings,
No movement made.
Yet upward soaring,
A gift God bestowed.
Effortless floating
Hundreds of feet high;
Rising thus in a moment.
So envious of your fly.
And my dream, "Why not I?"

July 1, 1975

– *8* –

I AM

I am the continuum,
Of five million years or more
From the oozing murky darkness,
Crawling to the shore,
Through countless mutant cycles
Of death and evolution,
Part fish, animal or fowl;
Reptile and mammal,
Earth, sea, and air,
Are elemental pieces of me.

I am the embodiment
Of my creator God.
Descending in myth
From a fallen Adam and Eve.
Clothed in this fragile body,
Knowing that Jesus, God's Lamb,
Walked this world like me.
Also Pilate and Judas
Within my shadow weave.

1976

– 9 –

A DEATH THAT SHOULD NOT BE

A death that should not be;
Says me.
My mind stumbles to reconcile;
Angry all the while
Life that was still to bloom;
Met its doom
Maybe we can never know;
Why God said – Go!
Years only increase the mystery;
Add to history
And leave me feeling small;
Six inches tall
This God that I cannot control;
Or even cajole
Holds my life in tender care;
I am aware
Can it be existence never ends;
Merely bends
Through the cosmos and all time;
In some unfathomed rhyme
Birth and death mere entrances;
Like leaping dances
Such faith at times is strained;
Aggrieved and tear stained
We, the living must always adjust;
To a body gone to dust
Yet that life gave ours more meaning;
Even been redeeming
Sadness must give way to celebration;
For this creation
I now know a little more of me;
Perceptively!
Intuitively-
Becoming more free.

1976

– 10 –

THE WATERING HOLE

Through each quiet window frame,
With powdery sprayed on snow,
Small twinkling light and candles came
Those seeking to make their tensions go.

The stained glass walls, and hand honed bars.
Tiffany lamps and greenhouse plants,
Those ornate trees with lighted stars,
And graceful wreaths with lights that dance.

Gifts exchanged, and happily shared
Glasses clink, with eyes touched with tears.
A workplace commitment is bared,
Much later, with true friends held dear.

Crackling fire and a people crush
Surface talk and holiday cheer.
Make time suspended, slow the rush,
To be alone, a Christmas fear.

From offices friendly veneer,
Bags holding gifts, clutter each chair,
One last drink, remembering the year,
Then home; through electric dark air.

At last, the rooms are all empty.
The hearth emits some heat unblown.
The hope, the joy, the energy,
Focused on a Love, scarcely known.

Christmas, 1982

– 11 –

RANDOM THOUGHTS - PERCHANCE

Are all of our lives, perchance?
With no rhythm of the dance.
Are the secret sins well known?
And thus judged afar, unknown.

Does the face that hides the clown;
Joy, holding the sadness down.
And this pain that burns within,
Fully drowned in each days' din.

If there be a good or bad,
That relates to glad or sad,
And sorting what is observed,
One wonders what is deserved.

This mind is clearly too small;
An infinitesimal ball.
Can anyone really know,
If this is a shadow show.

Should this life be fraught with fear?
Being scared for all held dear,
Or is it our history
To open each mystery.

Are mistakes always like death;
Or can revival with breath –
Feed and nourish heart and soul;
Push us towards a higher goal..

(continued)

RANDOM THOUGHTS – PERCHANCE (continued)

Each walk a separate road,
And carry a unique load.
Who is it can really say,
There's but a singular way.

May 10, 1982

– 12 –

"LA STRADA"

May rain
Umbrellas
The City gray
Puddles play
Scurrying energy
Keeping splash and spray
At bay.

Away from the damp
An open door – within
Soft Lamps
Dark mirrors
Smiling sounds
Over friendly sighs
Intimacy around
Relaxing the tightly wound
Nourish outside and in.
Small rays – fresh glow
A piece of essential soul.

May 23, 1989

– 13 –

FALL AND WINTER

The purple of the mountain shade,
Stars, first seen in the late day fade.
The dusting rusty leaves that blow,
The trickling rivers' subdued flow.

That orange white crackle like a flame
The falling signs of change that came.
Earth prepares its annual repose
Resting the heart in winters' shadows.

Glistening golden yellows in time,
Soulful reeds, caught bending in rhyme,
Spraying dusty delicate snow,
Against the path that I must go.

Racing toward the twilight shade,
Natures' melody yet to fade.
The vision in this winter's night,
Grace and balance, a halo of light.

Christmas, 1990

– 14 –

SVOBODU
(FREEDOM)

Blackness surrounds this sphere of blue and white,
Consciousness of all, forever transformed,
Focuses vision on an image of light;
Show how fragile, how unique, how slight.
Appearing so calm, it beckons, it invites,
And we are entwined in setting new sights.

Yet the world has waited in uneasy camps.
Conflicts flared and tensions like lamps
Caught in an invincibly strong squall,
Flickered or roared, but always a pall.

Then the change! The people arose,
By saying, "enough!", and bravely opposed
The choking state. The 'invincible' might.
Walls and barriers fell at the sight
Of candle lit marches, shouting "svobodu".
Old order shrivels, gives breath to the new.

The journey has begun; the result not yet known,
There's enough tinder, and sparks to be blown.
But maybe, just maybe, this sphere in the black,
Has taken a turn, toward a peaceful tack.

Christmas, 1990
(Svobodu - Hungarian)

– 15 –

FUTURE THOUGHTS

As grandchildren are born each year,
All of them, my heart holds most dear.
I began to wonder what would they see,
As they travel through the next century.

They will not know, there was once no TV;
Or jets, computers, or micro-surgery.
With the wars like 'Nam so dim in the past,
Or the struggles of blacks, winning at last.

Yet changes for them, will follow apace,
Awareness begun with a view from space,
That focused our essence as one human race.
Stuck on an Island, fragile as lace.

Surely sources of energy, unknown to us,
Power our planet, and not be ruinous.
And they will, I guess, travel in space;
Far corners of Earth will be commonplace.

Paradigms we know will surely shatter,
Change the knowledge of existence of matter.
They well may see five generations,
With an expanding of life's expectations.

Still mysteries of values and soul will confound,
Danger and terror will still be around.
Yet as expansive as our mind can be,
We have only look backward to clearly see,
How impossible for any to really know,
The amazing changes the future will bestow.

Late Fall, 1990

– 16 –

GLASSMAKER

An art from the ages,
And a furnace that is new,
Skilled body; creative mind.
Each piece unique.
Starting tempo is slow,
The flow and the molten glow,
A twirl and roll,
An appliqué.
Help from another,
Is indispensable,
Strong hands
The rhythm and beat.
Melodic sounds and quick feet,
An ever present heat.
Feel and roll in opposing ways.
The culmination comes rapidly;
Quick spin – three thrusts,
Rapidly cut the chord,
What the mind has dreamed,
We now behold!

Christmas, 1992

– 17 –

THOUGHTS DRIVEN BY UNTIMELY DEATH

For certain, it is not fair,
This life ---
That takes from us
Those with so much to share.
Spent in their prime,
Leaving us wanting, and left behind.

With the cutting of the cord,
Frail sands commence their flow,
Drifting in infinite ways,
And we are not in control.

Logic searches for grand purpose,
Or hopes one is in play.
While feelings seek to find,
Answers – one at a time.

Humanity has braved this riddle,
During all of existence,
Witnessing, yet not perceiving.
Creating, throughout each age,
Structures for the mind and heart,
With scenarios designed to explain –
And somehow lessen the pain.

Celebration of life we can share,
Joy and grief; opposites we bear.
Teeming crowds are only fantasy.
Each path must be walked alone.
With the succor of fervent prayer;
We, in isolation, are left to trust.
Sight unseen, that all is just.

(continued)

THOUGHTS DRIVEN BY UNTIMELY DEATH (continued)

My body is but the carrier,
Around this earthly crust.
In time, battered and bust,
Resulting in my eventual dust.

In this existence, vaguely aware;
Of what I am or might be.
But a living lasting legacy,
In mind and soul and grace,
Floats free, exquisitely…

Summer, 1994

– 18 –

SUMMER STORM

Summer stillness fills the valley,
Foggy mist hugs the hillside,
Deer have begun their evening graze,
Campers singing around a fire,
Toasting sweetness on a stick.

The darkness is now closing in,
Above the trees, the thickening clouds,
Breezes blow and brightened blaze,
A far distant rumble portends.
The grazers abandon the field,

A flashing bolt crests the black hill,
Logs and people in sudden scatter,
Wind grows wilder, flashes brighter,
The thunder fills the sturdy house,
And rain plummets the old tin roof.

The full fury of this eerie night,
Is all about us in the now,
With cracks, and flashes, and wind.
Safe for now, within thick brick walls,
Each mind filled with awe and wonder.

Summer, 1996

– 19 –

WHERE IN THE WORLD

If I were ever dropped from a cloud,
And put in a spot to make my way,
I might decide to hide in a crowd,
Or just rest, close by a pristine bay.

Dreaming of places, I just might choose,
My mind leaps to some that make me dance.
Hoisting sail for a warm gentle cruise,
A Rio night to begin romance.

The village of Grachen in silent repose,
Crisp night air, a fireplace blazing,
Steep alpine slopes, their grandeur impose,
Sounds of bells from cattle grazing.

Maybe Scotland's hills, hearty folks chose,
Colorful heather and fences of stone,
Scattered pubs, cordial people enclose,
Regal cities, to descry alone.

Coolness and green with snowcapped peaks,
This jewel, this Isle, like Eden's doorway.
The seasons reversed, and English speaks,
Pulsing vigorous people at play.

Choosing one special place to reside,
Where being there, could make me whole.
My flights of fancy and real collide,
It's in Salzburg, to immerse my soul.

Fall, 1996

– 20 –

REVERIES OF LOVE

The throbbing magic from the start,
Heavy heart, at being apart,
One presence and the room is filled,
Together and the world is stilled.
A special writing just for you,
Glances only fathomed by two.

To know this person in every way,
With growing trust built day by day,
Caring so much for someone's life
Through the happiness and the strife.
And though we grow in distinct ways,
The journey of life enriches our days.

From each birth you see them grow.
Investing everything you know.
Dawning young, helpless, in need;
Precious lives you nurture and feed.
A lifetime of sharing the sad with tears,
Hopes, dreams, plus laughter and fears.

A small hand that reaches to hold,
Moments together, rich as gold,
Skipping along the rustic lanes,
Memories, the heart always retains.
Hugs and tugs and being with you,
Then "I love you", from out of the blue.

November, 1996

– 21 –

LOVE COUPLETS

Grandpop's trip to the park with me,
Watching some baseball at his knee.

The beginnings of life with a mate
Where days and nights like one long date.

Love that slowly grows to be
An affirming, 'I love me.'

Love that came out of the blue,
When troubled waters were the cue.

Inner love a father knows
While watching his children grow.

Even love that comes from reaching out
Knowing what a stranger is about.

Love experienced in unexpected ways
As risking, trusting, sharing pays.

Love of a friendship lately regained
After years of shunning silence pained.

Experiences in our camping van
Warmth of love shared within our clan.

October, 1997

– 22 –

ANGEL AMONG US

'Tis said that all angels have wings.
I can tell you they're some that don't
One of the mysteries life brings,
My heart can see what my eyes won't.

Possession of an inner light,
And dwelling here with me and you.
Perceptiveness, from a great height,
And a caring and loving view.

Even when times are less than right,
This angel inspires a trust,
And through the turmoil shows what might
Come true from a spiritual lust.

So this ongoing presence with me,
In God's unique way of showing,
I'm not cast adrift in the sea,
And my soul is stronger, knowing.

Christmas, 1997

(written in memory of the Rev. Joey Noble,
who passed much too soon)

– 23 –

LAZY BAY DAY

It's a summer lazy Bay day,
Triangles of white skittering like bugs,
Above are puffs of light to gray
Rolling, rolling, in endless array.
And the ripples on the water
Reflect the doldrums of the wind.
The canvas flaps and strains.
No other sounds but gulls and cranes.
The mind is drifting far, far away,
To different times. Different days.

Where the wind raged and churning water foamed,
When sails were taut and true danger roamed.

And to a time on a high mountain road,
Narrow and deep, with a delicate load.

To a sparkling night when the Southern sky
So heavy with stars, brought a we filled sigh.

To a busy harbor at the setting sun,
Blending turmoil, of God and man as one.

Christmas, 1998

– 24 –

A DREAM

I row alone in the misty dark.
Undirected, but with no fear,
The gentle waves lap the sides
And nothing in this world seems near.

Then rising massively ahead
Are piers of concrete and steel.
Surely for a bridge and yet
Nothing of the sort is clear.

Now as I come ever so near,
From the dark, a door appears.
I leave the boat adrifting there.
The door gives way to pulls and tugs
And gives me leave to enter in.

A sound of gentle closing behind,
Ahead, a large staircase beckons,
Wide, so grand, and palatial;
Richly robed in royal red
And spiraling, spiraling, down.
Large torches fill walls with light,
And I am drawn to explore.

Following where I cannot see.
Sounds faintly drift to my ears
Sweet erotic, uniquely upbeat.
A sense of joy floods my heart
And my quickened steps are sure.
I lean to glimpse the floor below;
Music rolls and the crowd is swaying,
I leap and join the dancers below.

Christmas, 1998

– 25 –

SOME MUSINGS

What I don't understand
Would fill many thick books.
It begins with this life,
And why its given to me.
Is it being squandered
Or is it what I am meant to be.
Do I have any real control?
Or are my actions just scripted
And while I think I am free
My mind is far too small to see.
Next, this thing about a true God.
A being's universality
Where humans long for a sense
That somewhere exists an order
Unfathomable and unclear.
And then there is this tiny speck,
The one we have known as Earth.
Will we survive our basest selves?
Or disappear in an inglorious end?
Then I wonder in this infinite expanse
That grows without our knowing,
And as complex a species as we
May pale if all were made clear.
That on many particles of cosmic dust
Are others more developed than us.

Christmas, 1999

– 26 –

MISS JOAN

Do you have a moment to hear
A story of a very special life?
Of a woman who flowed against the tide,
Who from the earliest of her days,
Seized her time and began a ride.
And those that tried to match the pace
Often fell breathless on their side.
It was every instant that defined the race.

Thinking back to those early years.
Solid with instilled immigrant dreams,
Deep faith in God, as a voice to hear,
Plus all the hope, pain, joy, and fear.

A time to think and choose a career.
Then an abrupt change in life,
When a tall man entered the scene,
And love and marriage was to intervene.
But if you thought life's pace would slow,
The essence of Joan, you just don't know.
For every day, there were new seeds to sow.
Three girls born and raised to fly.
A solid rock, an anchor, a guy.

The years produced and endless array
Of stories; telling this or that foray.
For clearly she had a wonderful trait,
To love and laugh, and often tempt fate.
And you could spend many a night
Recounting Joanisms, that made our days bright.

(continued)

MISS JOAN (continued)

Shocked by the suddenness with which life went down,
Yet with courage, with grace; barely a frown.
This body, this shell, is all that died.
Her soul on an eternal heavenly ride!

July 20, 1999

(In memory of a dear friend, gone too soon.)

– 27 –

THE RITZ BAR

A spring storm with lightning bolts,
Wind driven rain on the tinted panes
Pleated, tightly drawn floral drapes,
Paneled walls, gilded landscapes
Animal sculptures and deep plush chairs,
A mood from soft-lit chandeliers.
Etching this piece of life's story,
And weaves into our memory.

Day is done, quiet hum of voices,
A piano sets a tone that rejoices,
Melody and beat hang in the air,
In background, but the mind is aware.
And tonight almost no one is here,
Yet a dream figure offers cheer.
A woman in red begins to croon
"As time goes by", an oldies tune.

Christmas, 2000

– 28 –

FAÇADE

In the middle of life's travel,
I'm careful to relate, not unravel,
The "me" you will see in measured sips,
On this journey of uncharted trips
Through life's ways; a winding maze.
This façade a product of countless days,
Of learning, drive by unfathomed pain,
Spent soaking in the icy rain.

The risks I see are very real,
And cut to the fabric of my being.
If it's the veneer you wish to peel
From the persona that you are seeing,
Chipping away at this hardened crust;
I must sense and feel a knowing trust.

Fall, 2002

– 29 –

THE WINE BAR

Tables and seats are nearly empty,
The sun sits in the afternoon sky,
Walls are fully covered with wine,
Menus are not yet complete.
Anticipation of the night to come,
And the staff is congregating.

Now the regulars start to arrive.
And a cheery hum of joy grows.
A bubbly Bellini to start,
It's Friday, the work week is done.
Measured glasses carefully poured.
And the menus tempting delights
Chosen not to overwhelm,
Perused between swirls of red or white.

Those earthy smells of berries and soil,
Sips savored and opinions shared.
Now there is twilight without,
Time has a way of drifting away,
And the dimming lights enhance the feel.
Patrons flow on in, two by two.
Fill the aisles and quietly wait.

Labels read and bottles caressed,
The food aroma adds subtleness,
Light fare mixed by classy dishes.
When the last glass has been drained,
And the chosen bottles are boxed,
We bid goodbye and head away,
Vowing to very soon, return.

Christmas, 2005

– 30 –

HAUNTING

I am a very lonely man,
Wandering through an endless land.
Searching through the mysteries,
Garnered from our histories.

I want to live honest and free.
No elites deciding for me,
What it is I should think or do.
Their perverseness pushing a view.

I'm steeped in a reality,
Much in this world threatens me.
And the darkness of mankind's strife
Seeks to rob me of happy life.

Let none doubt the power of fear,
That can covet all you hold dear.
My lonely labor is to stay free,
And find a moral clarity.

There is a beacon that I see.
It shines to mark our destiny.
It grew from fertile minds set free,
And built on tensions of you and me.

Epilogue

It's freedom's song that we all sing,
And Liberty's bell we all ring.
We are blessed/cursed with our power.
The World needs us in this dark hour.

Christmas, 2007

– 31 –

PURSUING THE DREAM

Pursuing the dream;
One human matters
One moment in lights;
Endless waves of thunder
Acknowledged as the best;
Of any living on Earth.
For now – a glow.
For life – the memory,
Forgiven – the pain
Salved with Olympic gold.

Fall, 2008

– 32 –

SOLITUDE

The window frames two trees,
Late November, still with leaves,
The sky is eerie dark,
Lightning flashes glow,
Distant light of a setting sun;
There is a house nearby.
Wood debris clutters the ground.
The deck is wet with leaves,
Dying Mums still decorate.
Junk remains from summer fun.
In the den, its football on TV.
And sounds of cheering are heard.
While in my solitude,
Warm behind the curtain lace,
Near a crackling fireplace
And the decorated Christmas horse,
Waiting for some child to mount,
To make a North Pole trip,
On which the mind will go,
Faded daisy Mums of yellow
Are encroaching on the window view,
And a solitary cat,
Stalks an imaginary foe.

Fall, 2008

– 33 –

DESTINY GONE

Don't you get angry? I know I do.
Of elites who know what's good for you,
What great insight gives them divine right?
That somewhere, somehow, they've seen the light.

It has all the basics of power,
To control your life and make you cower,
And then what happens to dissent,
Belittled, threatened, made to lament.

"Global Warming" is a raging case.
Conclusions reached with undue haste.
A religious aura at its worst,
Fear that any further truth will burst,
The real goal is furtively unfurled,
To tell us how to live in this world.

Our super strength thrust on us, unsought;
That conflagration far away wrought.
In the end there was just one choice.
To speak and act as freedom's voice.

And who might rise to take our place;
And seek to show an enlightened face.
Corrupted UN? China? EU?
How comfortable does that make you?

If we now relinquish our role,
Destiny gone; the death of our soul.
If a people won't fight to be free;
Left in the dust bin of history.

Winter 2008

– 34 –

THE ENDLESS PLAY
(PART 1}

The existence we all share is an endless play.
Each of us is inserted somewhere on the way.
Our destiny is to spend some moments on the stage.
We have our time; with lines just penciled on a page.

Our first appearance; crying helpless and afraid.
A blank tablet, though each one a miracle made.
And this stage we share, begets new life every day.
From that moment, we all move in a profound way.

Much is predicted by place and station of birth.
Maybe a land where human life has little worth.
Perhaps it is where the female remains repressed.
Or possibly where all of freedom is suppressed.

Mounting the stage; the individual role we play,
Is written or adlibbed for each and every day.
No one can be sure; or even foresee their lot,
About the way billions of souls will affect the plot.

While our tenure is measured and fleeting at best.
Even the least of us has some effect on the rest.
The cacophony of the crowd seems in disarray,
From chaos is created the threads of a play.

Fall, 2009

– 35 –

THE IRON BRIDGE WINE COMPANY

I park my car in the early fall heat
Anticipating my upcoming treat,
Entering, I glance to the bar.
Where an empty seat beckons afar.

The part cloudy late September light,
As cars whiz by on their homeward flight.
And tucked away in my high backed seat,
I watch across the fields of waving wheat.

I am looking at reds or whites to try,
So many choices from fruity to dry,
I choose a red with help from Nate,
His expertise has always proved first rate.

First the bar stools begin to fill,
Small talk and cell phones now appear,
Talking happily at the end of the day,
Stories and gentle patter hold sway.

Now the tables are filling with guests,
The day now done; relaxed and unstressed.
But over all it's wine that is King,
With choices, options, and smells and things.

The menu is full of unique light fare,
To complement wines, chosen with care.
And I peruse for just the right treat,
Some exotic fishes or savory meat.

(continued)

THE IRON BRIDGE WINE COMPANY (continued)

The clouds gently reflect the setting sun.
Soft light inside, enhance the real fun.
The walls are shelved with myriad wines
From the world over, yet similar vines.
The tastes of soils in faraway places,
Enhanced by care of cultural traces.

Early Fall, 2009

– 36 –

AGAIN

Is there no escape from elitist thought?
Oblivious of the chaos that's wrought.
The grab for power, the pompous vanity,
That they know what's best. It's insanity.
Through the ages, it is always thus,
Faux enlightenment, infectious pus.

The true arrogance of the ideas raised,
That fights all critique, a sameness view.
No search, no leeway, for what's said is "true".

It carries the burdens that religions' bore,
With dogma, shunning, persecution and more,
And exploitation to match evil intent.
Freedom and openness are seriously bent.

There are always times that masses will rise,
And throw off oppression that they despise.
The elites overreach; and disrespect,
In the mayhem, the citizens reject.
Once again, a fragile balance restored.
Vigilance is a must, forevermore.

Christmas, 2009

– 37 –

PRECIOUS

We go through life day by day
And never think along the way
It could be suddenly taken away.
How little we contemplate, 'What may',
A test and a comment made aside,
A concern, something wrong, inside.
How quickly, a roller coaster ride;
Answers I seek. And to run and hide.

And now this life, we take for granted,
Seems to be fleeing, a future tainted.
And I so much want to stay alive,
Much to do, much to strive.
Every moment, the prayer and hope,
Allow this cup; to let me cope.
Now this life I see as precious,
Savor each day, let it enmesh us.

And now there's news to give me joy,
The steps are hard, but I can employ,
To endure and steel forevermore,
No test or pain I can't endure.
The future; it appears is bright.
From the darkness into the light.
There will be no need to say,
"I wish I had done more each day!"

Fall, 2010

(This was written as a result of being diagnosed
wth rectal cancer in July, 2010)

– 38 –

EARLY WINTER

The purple of the hilly shade,
A twinkling star in the late day fade.
The dusty, rusty leaves that blow;
The trickling river's subduing flow.
The falling signs, different, yet same.
Cloudy sunset shows an orange like flame,
A part of earth prepares for sleep,
Resting its heart in winter's deep.

Glistening golden yellows of a time,
Soulful reeds, caught bending in rhyme;
Spraying the dusty delicate snow,
Against the path that I must go.
Racing towards the twilight shade
Before the melody starts to fade;
The vision seen in this winter night;
Beauty and balance, slivers of light.

Christmas, 2013

– *39* –

MEMORIES – 1955

A young officer starts to embark,
On a trip that leaves a lasting mark.
My ancestors land in deep disgrace,
With wonder and nerves racing apace.
Others with me must be feeling alike,
As we board the DC-3 this night.

It's twenty-four hours in the sky,
Two stops for gas and resupply.
So slow, so low, and Spartan seats.
Sleep is sporadic amid motor beats.
At last a landing near the Main,
Nothing to see from the plane.

To a bus and highway flow,
Then an 'ESSO' sign aglow.
Traffic streams on hubs and spokes,
Past dark homes gray like smoke.
And now the city is ablaze,
Bright lights and colored neon rays.

An old hotel on a darkened street,
The stark clean room seems a suite.
What sights will tomorrow bring,
The mind has trouble imagining.
In no time, a deep weary sleep,
So fast, no need for counting sheep.

(continued)

MEMORIES – 1955 (continued)

Arising to a crisp late fall morn,
To see firsthand, this land of scorn,
The Bahnhof rises with a short stroll,
A massive hub, nary a bullet hole.
Abundant cars and teeming stores,
Far removed from war torn sores.

Fall, 2014

– 40 –

BIG BAND DREAM

Sixteen musicians fill the stage,
A dance band from another age.
In Army dress from World War II,
Brass, piano, saxophones too.
And the music that fills the room,
Is "String of Pearls" an old heirloom.

And yet my mind is drifting away,
Another venue, distant day.
A time; a young man and his wife,
At the start of their married life,
With the Army across the sea,
Searched for New Year's festivity.

In our Volkswagen bug of blue,
Speeding to bid the year "adieu".
The Wiesbaden O club, our goal
Where "Glenn Miller Band", set to roll.
The lights dim, the music begins,
The sound excites the soul within.
The floor is filled with happy pairs,
"Moonlight Serenade" fills the air.

We cannot imagine where else to be,
Lively music, my wife and me.
All too soon, the clock unwinds
And then "Auld Lang Syne" fills our minds.
Balloons fall and kisses abound,
What new hopes and dreams will be found?

(continued)

BIG BAND DREAM (continued)

Bouncing home on slick cobblestones,
The winter moon, shining full-blown.
Winding the hilly countryside,
A warm glow on the pair inside,
A New Year day will quickly dawn,
Where possibilities are born.

Christmas, 2015

Afterword

– *1* –

INDIAN RESERVATION

Sandy, barren, useless land,
Sage and scrub brush survive,
Cruel hot sun beats the sand.
Hopelessness stenches the air.
Terrain dotted with mud baked huts,
Or small shacks, one step removed.
Skinny goats search patches of green.

Beneath floppy roadside canvas
Forlorn scene of selling beads,
Marginal gain at best.
Dry heat leathers the skin.
Huddled aged and youthful kin.
Choking dust upward swirls,
People scratching existence there.

Banished to unwanted lands,
Victims to the Western push.
Herded, forgotten and alone.
All of us a bit less free,
While our Indians stay in misery.

January, 1974

– 2 –

ALONE

Oh! In a crowd
To scream out loud –
I need! I need!
Will you not come
To soothe my soul,
Leaden and bowed.

To be alone
And feel the ache
I sometimes think
My heart will break!

March, 1972

– 3 –

WAKE UP

This land you thought would be forever free,
Is slipping very close to tyranny,
And if your willful blindness cannot see,
A once great country will be history.

Fall, 2014

– 4 –

THE CASTLE OF MY BEING

The castle of my being,
Is built with unhewn rock,
And while it seems craggy rough,
It shoulders abundant spirit,
Against the whispers of control.

Christmas, 2015

– 5 –

WINTER'S DAY DAWN

The trees are barren and stark,
And beneath an early frosty fog,
Coats the forest meadow bed,
Distant voices and a dog bark,
Announcing winter's day dawn.

Christmas 2015

– 6 –

LIFE'S JOURNEY

This journey we travel during a life,
Goes on forever. It never ends;
This earthly body suffers much strife,
But eternity does not break. It bends.
We must all face a steep, winding climb,
So that our soul is free to grow.
When the hereafter becomes or time.
Gratefully, we almost never know.

March, 2014

(Sent to a friend facing death)

– 7 –

THE ROOF

The canyon creek, the wind pocked walls,
Quiet light from the crescent rays,
Countless stars in random arrays,
Create the roof that ends my days.

Fall, 2008